MW00931592

The Millennial Way Home
An Invested Millennial Guide on buying Your First Real Estate Property

Jeremy Kho

BE IN CONTROL OF YOUR FINANCIAL FUTURE AND START YOUR INVESTING JOURNEY TODAY

Check out the course on becoming an Invested Millennial

<u>The Invested Millennial Money Management Course</u>

(http://tinyurl.com/investedmil)

Join us today!

Contents

Introduction

Are you considering buying or investing in real estate? There are some points you should consider before you begin, which could decide whether you succeed or fail with real estate investing.

Prior to any investment in real estate, you need to think, can you afford it? After all, buying real estate is an expensive venture to get into, and you need to look at your budget.

If you have to take out a mortgage loan to buy the investment property, can you afford to pay the loan back? It's a big commitment, and you need to decide whether you can afford it before you begin.

What is the reason that you are buying or investing in a home? Are you buying for your personal use and for your family? Or are you buying for the sole purpose of reselling or renting it?

If the building is a home for you to stay in, you should check the basics and walk through the house and talk to the neighbors to ensure that it meets your needs.

If you are buying a home to resell it in the future, find out how much the land is likely to appreciate, and research which areas are going to bring you the best profit. It's vital to know these facts as you do not want to end up buying a home that is unlikely to be in demand.

The next point to consider before investing in real estate is choosing a good agent. When you choose an agent, go for one who has good market knowledge, and who knows the latest trends in the market.

This book, as written from a millennial perspective, will run you through the basics that you need to know in owning or investing in your first home.

Are you a First Time Home Buyer?

As a millennial, getting your first home can be quite exciting, and it can also be quite stressful. On top of the endless paperwork, there is a big learning curve, and for many, investing thousands of dollars as a down payment and committing themselves financially for 10-30 years is nerve-racking.

Luckily, the home buying process is made much easier by following a few pieces of advice.

Before starting, the best thing you can do is to get in touch with a well experienced, licensed, and qualified realtor. A good realtor saves you time, money, and headaches by asking all the questions that you never thought to ask. They will help you understand all the details of the paperwork and the contract.

A realtor will help you prioritize what's most important versus what's nice to have in a home. They show you through every step of the buying process.

Most first-time home buyers never get everything they want in their first home, but a realtor can help you find what you need, and answer questions such as:

- Do you qualify for a loan?

- What are your affordability limits?

- Which programs do you qualify for? (FHA loan, down payment assistance, government grants, etc.)

- Which areas should you look at? (School zone, commute time to work, etc.)

- How big do you need your home to be? (Home layout, Number of bedrooms, etc.)

- What amenities do you need?

Only when you have a better understanding of what you need and want, will you stand a better chance of finding the home you need in your price range.

As well as finding an agent to help ease your stress, consider keeping your monthly expenses low. Try following the rule of 28/36. That rule is where you keep your total debt to income ratio below 36 percent and your total housing expenses to income ratio below 28 percent.

If possible, try to pay off, or reduce, any credit card debt, student loans, car loans, etc. Avoid opening new credit cards or retail store cards, or anything that can go on your credit report.

Before taking any action, seek advice from financial advisors to help you secure a favorable mortgage loan. Follow the rule of 28/36 and remember that you absolutely should not purchase a house you can't afford.

When you choose to purchase a house, you're making a huge step, and it's a hard choice. It's not hard because you don't have a clue whether you should or shouldn't buy. It's hard because you'll realize you're going to be paying a mortgage each month for the duration of the loan term, which commonly spans from 10 to 30 years.

The commitment is huge, and owning a home comes with some additional duties. For instance, you'll need to manage loan specialists, pay for property tax, pay for the house insurance, and then pay for any issues that may happen, for example, fixing a broken pipe or a broken electrical outlet. This is just the beginning, and yet it shouldn't stop you from purchasing a house.

You may be unsure whether you should choose to purchase or lease. The most important thing to note is, if you are buying the house, after the end of the loan term, you'll be the proprietor; else you'll need to pay a lease perpetually. However, that isn't always the case, which is why it is most important to understand the opportunity cost of leasing and your monetary goals.

What Your Buyer's Agent Not Telling You

As highlighted previously, an experienced, licensed, and qualified realtor can save you time, money, and headaches. But that's not always the case. Unfortunately, there are sneaky agents who claim that they can help you, but in reality, they are just looking to get the commission.

This chapter will focus on how to identify them.

How do these bad agents masquerade as good ones?

The bad agent pretends to be a hard worker

If you hire a real estate agent, you want them to work hard for your money, and a good agent understands that. If your agent is wasting too much time pretending to work hard, then they won't have time to actually get you valuable information you need to make an informed decision. The moment the contract is signed, and the agent gets the commission, a bad agent will run to their next contact on their list and never want to talk or help you anymore.

Charmer

Every now and then, you'll meet the person who knows exactly what to say. They know the words you are looking to hear and which will make you feel comfortable in trusting them. When you're looking for an agent, don't look for how kind, gentle or witty they are. Look at their results. Why are you hiring them anyway?

Not providing enough information

Information is vital to enable you to make important decisions. There are agents that hide information to get you to make the decision to buy the house. To check that your agent is honest with you and providing you all the information you need, always have another reliable source to verify the information.

Always do your own research and investigate your agent's claims to verify them. Hire a third-party to inspect the house before you buy it. Or ask local authorities about the crime rate in the neighborhood. There may be things that the agents won't tell you, but you can find a way to look for all the hidden information yourself before you make that big decision.

Now, after all the discussions, you may start wondering whether you need an agent. With private home sellers, you do not. But homes where sellers have an agent, you will need a buyer's agent to protect yourself.

Finding the right real estate agent.

Below is something to note, which will help you think more deeply before taking the plunge and hiring the right agent.

"My fees are negotiable."

Real estate agents always want to earn a bigger share of the pie so they won't tell you that you can actually negotiate for lower fees. Likewise, there may be other fees that your agent isn't telling you about.

There may be administrative fees or handling fees that you have to pay on top of your agent's commission. Knowing that you can negotiate on all of these fees can help lower the price of the property you're about to buy. Read and check the contract. There may be something there that you can negotiate and save you some money in the process.

"This house has termites. The park will be removed. The crime rate is high here."

Agents always talk about the positive features of the house, also inquire about the negatives. Do your own research. Find out who its previous owners are and spend some time in the neighborhood.

I'm sure you wouldn't want to live in an area where a drug dealer is going to be your neighbor or where the park that your children can go to will be eventually removed.

"There are other offers made for this house, and yours is the highest."

Agents usually favor buyers they can get the biggest commission from. If your offer is the highest without you knowing it, this can be both good and bad, depending on how you view things.

The good side is that you are likely to be awarded the house. However, the bad side is that you may actually be paying more than you should. Agents won't tell you whose side they're on, so it pays to do some research about the actual market value of the property.

"The chandelier is not included in the sale."

Get everything in black and white, read the contract thoroughly. The house may be furnished when you viewed it during the open house, but not everything that you've seen will be included in the sale.

Have a checklist included in the contract, so you know which things are going to stay and which of the items will be removed. This way, you won't get a shock when you move in and find that the beautiful chandelier is gone.

You can take a couple of steps to find the right agent to work for you. First, start by thinking of it as if you are trying to find an employee for your business.

Then have interviews with multiple agents and ask questions, including asking about their years of experience and the type of references they have. You can check with the Association of Real Estate License Law Officials, and you will be able to inquire whether the agent has any disciplinary actions filed against them and if they do what the action is about.

To Buy or Rent? That is the Question.

Your lifestyle is particular to you and your family. The questions that are shown below are aimed at understanding your lifestyle. Are you capable of repairing things around the house, or would you prefer to call the landlord or a superintendent to do the repairs? With a rental, you can give a lot of responsibility to someone else rather than fixing it yourself.

Could you actually manage your household better than someone else? Are you organized? Do you prioritize well? Do you manage your time well? Do you prefer to be in control of your living space or will anything do? You will probably prefer to own your own place, rather than renting if you like to be in control of your own space.

If you have a specific view of how you want your home to look, you'll probably also prefer to own it. If you want to alter things to your taste in a rental you need permission before you can do it and the owner may not want you to proceed.

The next important consideration is how long are you going to stay at your place? If you're unsure or time is short, it may be better to rent as going through the rigmarole of buying the property may not worth the effort.

What are the Numbers?

There seems to be a constant and heated argument on whether renting or owning is better. Whatever your preference, you should always know the numbers and compare both options.

The rental numbers include the rent and any possible bills you expect, including initial costs such as a possible rental broker fee and usually a landlord's security deposit.

With buying, you need to include the bills, property taxes, any required insurances, and the mortgage. Initial costs could also include a deposit, closing fees, and other costs such as renovation.

Usually, owning has more numbers to include than renting. Unlike owning, when it comes to rental, you do not make any gain or loss on the property when you move out. Any gain or a loss you make when you sell a house depends on the length of time you've owned the house, how you may have upgraded the house, and the market when you come to sell it. That means it's best to have an estimate of the selling costs if you want to make a realistic comparison between owning and renting.

Household maintenance and renovation costs are often forgotten, and these costs will occur if you own your own home, and they can be quite significant.

How the numbers change

You need to examine each scenario carefully. The first neighborhood you look at might be very expensive to buy in, yet the rent is comparable to elsewhere. In another neighborhood, the reverse could be true. Each scenario will yield different results, and it may be that the purchase price is actually lower than renting.

The numbers will also change if you're able to get a mortgage at a lower interest than was possible previously or is likely in the future.

Currently, most interest rates are low and are predicted to go higher. Currently, and for the next 5 to 10 years, utility costs will tend to rise faster than most other bills because of infrastructure improvements. Property taxes will also rise more quickly because governments are short of money.

Rent is likely to rise steadily too. If real estate prices crash, rent tends to rise due to more buyers becoming renters. If real estate markets soar, the lack of affordability will keep some people renting. When fewer houses are being constructed, because people can no longer afford the purchase prices, the lack of supply can also increase rents.

Should you buy or should you rent? Make sure you do your homework and tailor the decision to your life's needs. Remember that a decision you made 5 years ago may have to be reviewed and changed today, and the factors may have to be revisited to see how they have changed.

Understanding Opportunity Cost of Buying Versus Renting

Most investors involved in property investing understand the opportunities to make money through leverage and capital growth or high yields. However, many do not fully understand the concept of opportunity cost.

The encyclopedia definition says, "Opportunity cost is a term used in economics, to mean the cost of something in terms of an opportunity forgone (and the benefits that could be received from that opportunity) or the most valuable forgone alternative."

As an example, a city might decide that it wants to construct a hospital on one of the vacant plots that it owns. The opportunity cost is what could have been done with the land and with the funds used for building the hospital instead.

By building the hospital, the city has forgone the opportunity to build another facility on its land. Instead of a hospital, the city could have built a parking lot, a park or a sports center. They could even have sold their land and used the money to pay off part of the city's debt.

So, in property investing terms, if an investor decides to invest $50k in a property in for example Wales, the opportunity cost would be what they could have made by investing in Spain, Texas or Dubai.

If that investor decides to keep their $50k in stock equity, the opportunity cost is what they could invest their money using alternative investment vehicles that could yield better results.

Suppose that an investor is willing to increase his investment to increase his accumulation of wealth. That investor will have to divert resources away from other purposes, to acquire a real or another capital asset.

Therefore, the opportunity cost that the investor must bear is the loss or gain they would have received by investing the money elsewhere in the most valuable alternative.

Opportunity cost does not necessarily need to be in monetary terms. In fact, it can be in terms of anything that the investor values. The consideration of opportunity cost is one of the key differences between the concepts of economic cost and those of accounting cost.

Assessing opportunity cost over a scale of values to investors is the basis for deciding the true costs of any decision.

When there is no explicit accounting or price attached to a course of action, ignoring opportunity cost may produce the illusion that the benefits derived from a certain course of action cost nothing at all. The unseen opportunity cost then becomes the hidden cost of that course of action.

It is important to note that opportunity cost is not the sum of all available alternatives, but it is instead the benefit that could have been derived by opting for only the best alternative.

The opportunity cost to a real estate investor might be the benefit foregone by not investing their capital into stocks, or in a different property, or not at all (as in the case of an investment resulting in a capital loss for example).

Save Money by Renting instead of Buying a Home

In the continuing debate over the benefits of renting against buying a home, those who support ownership of your own home always claim that when you pay your mortgage, you're paying yourself each month and building up your equity.

What they forget to think about is that the money they save from renting, they could be paying themselves a whole lot more.

Here's an example of a renting versus buying scenario:

Let's say that the Brown's purchase a home for $200,000 in 1998 and put a deposit of $20,000 down. In ten years, after a housing boom, their home is worth $350,000. Their house has appreciated at a rate of around 5% per year.

While the Browns got a few tax savings thanks to owning their own home, they also paid around $2000 a year for insurance and another $2000 for property taxes. And they pay a further $2400 each year to maintain the house in good condition.

Their utility bills also cost around $100 a month ($1200/year) and, of course, they have to pay their mortgage interest.

If they had a 30-year mortgage at a 7% interest rate and the inflation rate was 3.5$, and their capital appreciation was calculated, the Browns would pay about $107,000 to live in their home for 10 years.

Now, using a basic rental calculator will tell you that had the Browns rented a similar house for around $1200 a month, and paid the same for utilities and insurance each year, their rental would have cost them roughly $157,000 to live in their home for 10 years.

What the basic rental calculators don't tell you is what would have happened had the Browns invested their $20,000 down-payment into a mutual fund or a Guaranteed Investment Certificate (GIC) and invest their extra monthly amount of $800 to $1000 into other low-risk investments.

Well, let's find out.

Comparing Rental and Buying with Other Investments

Putting their money into a high-interest saving account or a Guaranteed Investment Certificate at 4% and by investing $800 a month, and keeping the rest of the extra money for fun and entertainment, their savings would amount to nearly $157,000 after ten years.

Subtract that small investment income from the Brown's rental living costs for the last ten years ($157,000), and that means that the Browns had broken even. Diversifying their investments or by making more adventurous investments, they might have made considerably more.

Buying a new home is very appealing. However, it's important that you do the math. Doing the math is particularly important when you're purchasing a home is a depreciating market or a market that is not appreciating at the rate that gives a good return.

In the past, homes have usually appreciated in value at a reasonable rate. However, this is not guaranteed. In a depreciating housing market, homeowners and home investors can lose money.

There's no doubt that owning a home comes with its own great advantages, not the least of which include the ability to almost do what you want with it. You also have its potential as a good investment if you bought at the right time, in the right area and you keep a good grip on the longer-term costs of the house.

Remember, if your main view is on the overall financial value, don't discard rental as a viable option. Always do your math! And that's what separate an invested millennial from an average millennial.

Mortgages Available for You

Usually, you will need to get a mortgage for your first real estate investment. It's an important step, so make sure you look at all the available options. Naturally, having a good credit score helps. The better your credit is, the better the chances of you getting a loan that suits you. Several different kinds of mortgages are available; these are described below.

The Fixed Mortgage

The fixed rate mortgage usually lasts for 30 years, and the interest rate doesn't change, hence the term "fixed rate". This is the mother of mortgage loans. For a long time, real estate buyers could only get this type of mortgage.

Getting a fixed mortgage loan means that it has a fixed rate which remains the same all through the period of the mortgage, usually 30 years or it can be less if extra payments are made to pay off the loan more quickly.

At the end of 30-years, the mortgage is considered fully paid. In the initial years, each monthly mortgage payment is used to pay off the interest on the loan.

After some years, the mortgage payments are then used to pay off the principal balance. This is probably the most straight forward loan for buyers because the mortgage terms are very clear.

You don't normally hit any unexpected issue as you continue paying the loan off. Real estate buyers are likely to pay off the loan early so they won't be piled up with a great deal of debt for a long time and also paying more interest over the full term.

The Adjustable Rate Mortgage

Adjustable rate mortgage loans, also more commonly known as ARMs are nearly as popular as the fixed rate mortgages. By choosing this type of mortgage, you will have a varying interest rate.

A variable interest rate is the rate that lenders charge, and it often fluctuates. The rates change in accordance with the increase or decrease of interest rates in the market during that time.

An ARM usually starts with a fixed rate for a few years. Then it changes into a variable rate for the remaining period. This means that after the fixed rate period is over, the loan rate (and the monthly payment) is subject to adjustment every year. Most of the ARMs have a limit or cap on the amount they can charge.

Typically a 3/1 adjustable-rate mortgage is a 30-year mortgage that has a fixed rate for an initial three years then goes onto a variable interest rate for the final 27 years. Once the three-year fixed rate period is complete, the interest rate will be adjusted every year.

This type of loan can include a low-interest rate initially, and it is ideal for some buyers, particularly if they don't want to keep the property for the full term. In addition, if interest rates fall, they can grab the chance to get a new loan at a lower rate. However, if interest rates increase, they will have to go with the flow.

Unfortunately, ARMs aren't a sure thing because you don't know the amount of money you need to pay each month because the interest rate changes, which then affects your payment too.

No-Money Down Loans (Zero Down payment)

This is another kind of mortgage that buyers can obtain. They're sometimes advertised as one of the best loans around.

Real estate buyers can get this kind of loan by getting a 100% mortgage, or they can have a "piggyback" mortgage. The piggyback loan is where the buyer obtains two mortgages at the same time and puts them together. It is an additional loan beyond a buyer's first mortgage loan that is secured with the same lender.

With this, the buyer gets a benefit by not needing a down payment at the closing process. Also, a home buyer can benefit from getting the largest amount of interest available to include in their tax reduction.

You're not guaranteed to always get the entire amount financed in the mortgage. Many banks and lenders do not give the whole 100%. If they do decide to provide the whole amount, often it comes with higher interest rates.

The loan repayments will be more than the usual mortgage. This type of loan can hurt you in the longer term if you don't have quite a bit of money to pay the loan back. It would take you longer to have a comfortable cash flow because you would be paying a large number of loan payments. So, you might want to think long and hard about this loan option compared to your other options.

In short, a zero-down loan could still work out for you in terms of securing an investment property. It's up to you as to whether you're willing and able to take the risk.

Interest-only Loans

Another loan that is available for real estate buyers is the interest-only mortgage loan. Buyers can use this loan when they are having difficulty getting a cash flow that is solid and positive. This usually happens when the value of the property has increased, or if they're thinking about getting into property flipping at a future date.

When a buyer has this kind of mortgage loan, they can hold off on principal payments for a certain period. Usually, the period is no longer than ten years but could actually be less than that. The buyer is only paying the interest and nothing else during this period.

The principal remains outstanding until the period paying interest ends then the loan is amortized again. The buyer ends up paying a higher mortgage loan payment. There are several ways the buyer can handle this situation: sell their property, stick with the higher payment, or try to refinance.

As a millennial, you need to evaluate and estimate how your living expenses will change when you are getting your mortgage loan. Never commit to a mortgage loan that you can comfortably afford. Do not underestimate this as this will hurt you financially in short and long term.

Avoid being House Poor at all cost

Being house poor is nothing about the cost of your house. Your house might be absolutely wonderful and valued at $3 million, yet you are house poor if your home takes a disproportionate share of your income.

Normally, you're perceived as house poor if you devote too much on your house payments and house expenses. But what exactly is too much?

While there are several rules of thumb (Such as the rule of 28/36) that lenders use to calculate the reasonableness of your house costs, the actual property valuation and mortgage payment size is only part of the picture.

You're regarded as house poor if your property costs stop you from:

- Saving income to an emergency money reserve account (usually 3-6 months).
- Setting money aside for your retirement.
- Obtaining a diversified investment collection.
- Having money available for life events, such as paying for your child's degree.

- Choosing your new home's furniture.
- Only ever eating in your new kitchen.

To conclude, avoid the following mistakes.

- Buying a property that is more than you can afford.
- Buying property with No cash flow.
- Not understanding the expenses.
- Not keeping cash or reserve funds.
- Being in a rush to buy and doing little or no research.
- Getting the wrong loans or financing.

Do some quick planning when you start thinking about buying a new home and check the math to prevent becoming house poor. Talk to a financial professional to help you define your objectives and formulate a strategy for meeting them. Examine your budget with an eye toward trimming discretionary expenditures and saving more toward your objectives.

When you go through the loan pre-approval process, see the amount you qualify for on the basis of just your typical yearly earnings, without considering overtime, bonuses, part-time employment, or alimony or any other extra income you might receive. By doing that you may be unable to afford a big mortgage as you might like, but you will be in a much better position to pay off the loan against your home. Plus you'll avoid the stress of constantly juggling your finances.

Be very careful about using imaginative financial measures, such as interest-only mortgages or optional ARMs, because you could end up with a home that is actually unaffordable.

If home value increase or decline and interest rates rise, you might find yourself caught trying to make the mortgage payment each month and being unable to sell the house for enough to cover paying back the mortgage that secures it.

The bottom line for first-time millennial home buyers' is don't lose your home to property foreclosure just because you bit off more than you can chew, or in event that you can afford to buy the "Luxury" house, but don't do it just because society expects you to.

The Millennial Way Home

Here're the steps when it comes to getting your first real estate property.

- Decide which option is best for you? Buying a House or renting one? How will this decision affect you financially?

- Find out how much house you can afford, by considering your household expenses and household debt. Obtain your credit reports and find out your credit score. A good credit score will help you get a good rate when negotiate with a lender.

- Find a reputable buyer's agent and start looking for houses. The agent is going to represent you and your interests, the agent will work you through and finding the house you want.

- Find and choose a lender (banks and mortgage banks that provide the best rates) that will be providing a mortgage for buying your home. Get pre-approved letter for the mortgage loan.

- Find the house that you like and make an offer. You may need to hire a real estate attorney to understand the legal document you will be required to sign. When the offer is accepted, you'll need to deposit a percentage of amount as good faith money.

- Consider hiring a third-party home inspector, they will help to identify any potential major problems. Attain an appraisal from your lender on the house which protect the lender from over lending for a house. Prepare to negotiate with the seller after the inspection and appraisal.

- During the process, you'd want to purchase homeowner insurance. The insurance can be acquired separately or by the lender. Payments made to a homeowner's insurance policy are usually included in the monthly payments of the homeowner's mortgage.

- Closing the deal and signing the contract for the purchase of your home. Run through your settlement statement thoroughly before closing the deal. Understand the breakdown of fees, charges and funds on your end. Review it with your attorney so you are clear on everything.

Get the tools to access your home affordability from the link below,

https://tinyurl.com/1stHomeCalc

- Rent VS Buy Calculator
- Home Affordability Calculator
- Fixed Mortgage Loan Calculator
- Flexible Rate Mortgage Loan Calculator

Rent VS Buy Calculator

Rent vs. Buy Calculator (Max 30 Years)						
How Long Do You Plan to stay?	30	Years				
Buy Option				**Rent Option**		
Purchase price	$400,000.00			Cost of renting similar home		$1,800.00
Downpayment	$60,000.00			Broker's Fee		$1,000.00
Closing Costs %	3.5 %			Security Deposit		$2,000.00
APR	5.00%			Assumed rental price inflation		3%
Loan term (Years)	30			Assumed annual return on cash		8%
Property tax rate	1.25%					
Annual Utilities & Maintenance	$2,400.00					
Annual insurance	$1,200.00					
Assumed annual appreciation	4.00%					
Assumed marginal income tax rate	20%					
General inflation	3%					
Transaction Rate of Selling	6%					
Closing Fees	$14,000.00					
Mortgage Loan Amount	$340,000.00					
Monthly mortage payment	$1,815.45					
Home value after X years	$1,325,399.21					
Mortgage Loan Remained	$0.00					
Home Equity after X years	$1,325,399.21					
Initial Cost of buying	$74,000.00			Initial Cost of renting		$3,000.00
Total Montly Cost Spent for X years	$996,318.14			Total Montly Cost Spent for X years		$1,048,926.39
Transaction Cost of Selling	$79,523.95			Oppurtunity Cost (Initial Amount)		$776,436.81
Net Cash Earned from Selling	$1,245,875.25			Oppurtunity Cost (Buy vs Rent Diff)		$219,327.20
Net Proceeds	$175,557.11			Net Proceeds		-$56,162.39

Description:

This calculator helps to compare the costs of renting to the costs of buying a home.

Home Affordability Calculator

Home Affordability (By 28/36 Rule)					
Your Income			**Estimated Housing Expenses**		
Annual Income (Before Tax)	$60,000.00		Monthly Property Tax		$200.00
Total Debt to Income Ratio (1)	36%		Monthly Home Insurance		$75.00
Housing Expense to Income Ratio (2)	28%		Monthly House Utilities		$50.00
			Others Housing Expenses		
Current Monthly Debts Payment			Total Housing Expenses		$325.00
Student Loans	$250.00		PI Payment based on expenses (3)		$1,075.00
Car Loans					
Credit cards			**Your Available Funds**		
Others Loans			Available funds		$100,000.00
Total Current Monthly Debts	$250.00		Min Downpayment %		20 %
Max monthly housing payment (1)	$1,550.00		Closing Costs %		3.5 %
Max monthly housing payment (2)	$1,400.00		Home Price based on Funds		$425,531.91
Min of Criteria (1) & (2)	$1,400.00		PI Payment based on Funds (4)		$1,625.24
Your Financing					
APR	4 %				
Loan term (Years)	30				
Monthly PI Payment	$1,075.00				
Loan Amount	$225,170.83				
Available fund for downpayment	$89,003.88				
Estimated Closing cost	$10,996.12				
Maximum Home Price Affordable	$314,174.72				

Description:

This calculator helps to estimate the home affordability based on your income and your monthly debts.

Fixed Mortgage Loan Calculator

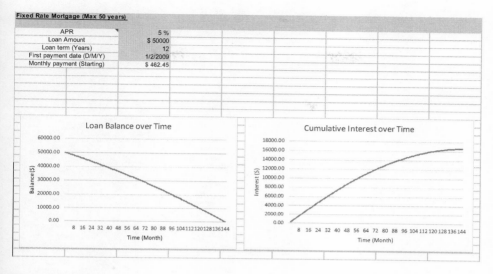

Description:

This calculator helps to analyse a fixed rate home mortgage.

Flexible Rate Mortgage Loan Calculator

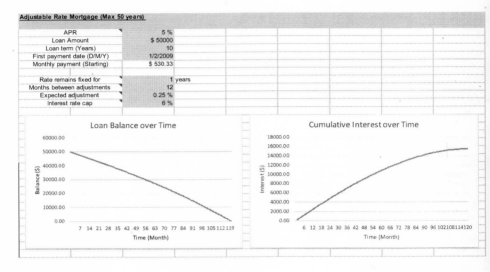

Description:

This calculator helps to analyse a variable rate home mortgage.

Bonus: Living A Life of Impact

"The only thing worse than being

blind is having sight, but no

vision."

Helen Keller

What's your career game plan? What's your business game plan? What's your life's vision? The Judaist King Solomon said, "Without a vision, the people perish". If you don't have a vision, if you don't have a game plan, you're going to have a hard time locating your provision. You've got to have a passion, a vision, something that drives you and keeps you going on. What do you see in your head each time you lay down to sleep at night? Where do you see yourself in 5 years, 10 years, 20 years?

Stop Chasing Money, Find Your Big Purpose.

There are three major forces reverberating through our world today, transforming everything they touch and creating unlimited opportunities for the creative minority. These three forces are: **the incredible growth in information, technology, and competition**.

Money is an instrument for transformation. The power it accrues is quite strong and forceful. We can even say without any doubt that money is the elder brother to change. Believe it or not, money changes things. Having it in profusion can affect a person's spirit, soul, and body positively. The lack of it can kill anyone's spirit as quickly as the wind will kill a lighted matchstick. However, you'll notice that, among these three forces, there is not one mention of money.

Yes! Money rules the world, money can help resolve your immediate financial insecurities, it makes things happen easily, makes immovable things to move, unstoppable things to stop, it's even said that lack of it; brings shame, weakness, disgrace, depression, hunger, fear, etc., but at what end? Life is not all about money. What then happens if you run out of this money? The point is, money is so powerful that everybody wants to have it. But, the factor is instead of chasing money day and night, working for someone; you should focus on finding your big purpose.

What Motivates You?

To be able to successfully achieve what you set out to do, you must find a motivating factor in that thing. Sidney Bremer speaking, said, "an intense desire itself transforms possibility into reality. Our wishes are but prophecies of the things we are capable of performing." Historians have said that it was Julius Caesar's red-hot desire and determination, rather than military skill that won his victories. So, when you set out to do the things that you are motivated to do, you are one step closer to achieving your desire. Motivation is a powerful tool; it is what we use to drive ourselves forward to complete responsibilities. There will be times when you feel drained, stressed and you want to give up. Then, the singular, red-hot desire which you have is what will motivate and keep you going.

Motivation for us can come in different forms. Our motivation may come from something tangible (physical) or something mental (psychology). Motivation for some people can be a selfish act. It depends on what they want to achieve with it. For other people, they are driven by an entirely unselfish and humane purpose. Motivation is driven by personality, skills, expectations, drive, ambition, gender, age, needs, wants, and as earlier stated, desires... but the list is endless.

Ordinary performers at work can accomplish extraordinary things through the power of desire; it's not enough to want a better business, promotion, and recognition. You have got to crave for it, reach for it, and pant for it. Let your desire for success motivate you, remember it is your responsibility to change your life from what it currently is to what you want it to be. Nobody can do it for you; people and things can only enhance the process, but in the end, your motivation has to come from within.

What is Your Ultimate Goal?

The crucial questions are: What is that one thing your life revolves around? What is that thing you will do anything to achieve, come hell or high water? What is your ultimate goal? As easy and straightforward as it may sound, many people still find it very difficult to answer this simple question. When asked a friend some time ago what his ultimate goal was, he had this to say, "My ultimate goal in life is to live a happy life, and this means working in a field I am passionate about, being financially secure, being healthy, and having ample free time to pursue my interests. I am very pleased with my current state of affairs, and so far, mission accomplished. That is kind of cool." Ask a lot of people and what you get is a similar response. The goals are the fuel in the furnace of success. A company or an individual without a goal is like a ship without a rudder. However, some people have an easy answer. For example, the billionaire, Warren Buffet, once said. "I always knew I was going to be rich. I don't think I ever doubted it for a minute". Others aren't as straightforward. Take Walt Disney, for instance, in the midst of several other successful people you can think of, it took a lot of time and effort before he got it together and became one of the most iconic people in the history of Hollywood. Right from the start, Walt Disney had his vision in perspective. His goal, which later translated to his company's mission statement is "...to be one of the world's leading producers of entertainment and information. Using our portfolio of brands to differentiate our content, services, and consumer products, we seek to develop the most creative, innovative and profitable entertainment experiences and related products in the world."

Walt Disney is one example of many. History tells the story of various people who got fired up with their goal so much that they changed the course of history. Henry Ford was passionate about producing automobiles. When he started out his company, he faced so many discouragements. He, however, believed so much in his vision. History has him today as the inventor of the earliest cars. Thomas Edison tried severally, and failed severally, to invent the light bulb. Eventually, he succeeded. Several others, including Michael Jordan, Milton Hershey, the world-famous renowned genius, Albert Einstein, Benjamin Franklin, Oprah Winfrey... the list is endless. All these great men and women had visions, set goals for themselves and they were passionate about their goals. The rest is history.

"Society has created a system to produce people who blindly follow the tide. It's time to break away from dogma and do what you love. "

Do you want to live a life of impact? Do you want to exist or truly live? What do you want to be remembered for? It's time for you to stop existing and start living truly. Now, find that one thing which you can die for and let the passion for it burn in you like fire. Then you'll stop existing and start living truly.

Disclaimer

This book and its contents are for general informational purposes only. It is not intended and as personal investment, tax, or legal advice, or recommendation. The book also should not be construed as an offer to sell or the solicitation of an offer to buy, nor as a recommendation to buy, hold, or sell any security.

The author is not a registered investment advisor, a registered securities broker dealer, or a certified financial planner, or otherwise licensed to give investment advice. The information and opinions provided in this book should not be relied upon or used as a substitute for consultation with professional advisors.

The use of or reliance on the contents of this book is done solely at your own risk. All opinions, analyses, and information included herein are based on sources believed to be reliable, and the book has been written in good faith, but no representation or warranty of any kind, expressed or implied, is made, including but not limited to any representation or warranty concerning accuracy, completeness, correctness, timeliness, or appropriateness.

In no event shall any reference to any third party or third-party product or service be construed as an approval or endorsement by the author. In particular, the author does not endorse or recommend the services of any particular broker, dealer, mutual fund company, or information provider.

About the Author

JEREMY KHO is a millennial in his early 30s. He is a self-published author, an individual investor, an engineer, and an online marketer. He had 5 years of experience in the consultancy firm in Singapore, and that experiences he acquired had helped him to think more logically and systematically in investing.

He had started his financial journey and investing in his early 20s, where he had been applying the same strategy in this Book. It is noteworthy that the strategy isn't some new idea – it's been advocated by many economists and investors, including Warren Buffett.

He had learned the idea on finances and investing during his career path, and he had learned from the books and courses on money matters, that with the correct money mindset, along with the knowledge and tool, toward financial freedom and a rich life is entirely possible.

Additional details about Jeremy, and the materials he offers can be found at:

Website   :Stress Proof Your Money

Facebook   :www.facebook.com/stressproofyourmoney

Twitter   :twitter.com/SProofYourMoney

More Goodies from Jeremy...

Course

The Invested Millennial Money Management Course

(http://tinyurl.com/investedmil)

Other Books

https://www.amazon.com/Jeremy-Kho/s?k=Jeremy+Kho

<u>Thank You for Reading My Book</u>

May I ask you a favor? If you got anything out of this book or if you have any comments. I appreciate all of your feedback and I love hearing what you have to say on the book.

Please leave me a helpful review on Amazon letting me know your thought. Your input will help make the next version of this book and my future books better.

Thank You!
~Jeremy Kho~

Made in the USA
Monee, IL
01 February 2021